Y0-AHH-923

The Sheep-Shearing

1762

A FACSIMILE PUBLISHED BY CORNMARKET PRESS
FROM THE COPY IN THE BIRMINGHAM SHAKESPEARE LIBRARY
LONDON
1969

PUBLISHED BY CORNMARKET PRESS LIMITED
42/43 CONDUIT STREET LONDON W1R ONL
PRINTED IN ENGLAND BY FLETCHER AND SON LIMITED NORWICH

SBN 7191 0193 X

THE
SHEEP-SHEARING:

OR,

FLORIZEL and PERDITA.

A PASTORAL

COMEDY

Taken from SHAKESPEAR.

The SONGS by Mr. *ARNE.*

LONDON:

Printed for J. TRUMAN, at SHAKESPEAR's
Head, in *Fleet-Street.*

MDCCLXII.

PROLOGUE.

TO raise the honour of the British stage,
   And swell the glories of ELIZA's *age,*
Great SHAKESPEAR *came, indu'd with ev'ry art*
To fire with rage, with pity melt the heart:
An early contract nature with him seal'd,
And, to her fav'rite, all her charms reveal'd:
Alike his skill, to paint the hero's woe,
Or bid the virgin's softer sorrows flow.
To draw young HARRY *in the fields of* FRANCE;
Or SHEPHERDS *gambols in the rural dance.*

The clown's coarse jests, the fortunes of a maid,
Whom nature's simple elegance array'd;
Princess, and milkmaid, and a prince's bride,
A subject for his WINTER'S TALE *supply'd;*
In which, the master-poet has interwove
The virgin innocence of past'ral love.

At ev'ry feast, to crown the rich repast,
The choicest fruits are always serv'd the last:
Stage cooks, indeed, reverse the bill of fare,
And ribaldry and farce, bring up the rear.

But for such guests as you, in whom we find
Judgment so clear, and taste so well refin'd,
A treat more delicate we wish to lay,
And SHAKESPEAR'S *wit shall send you pleas'd away.*

A

Dramatis Personæ.

POLLIXENES, King of *Bithynia*.

FLORIZEL, the Prince, his Son.

CAMILLO, a *Sicilian* Lord, in Banishment,

ANTIGONUS, a *Sicilian* Lord disguised as an old Shepherd, under the Name of ALCON.

AUTOLICUS, an arch Pedlar.

PAN.

CLOWN.

Priest.

PERDITA, supposed Daughter to ALCON.

DORCAS.

MOPSA.

Shepherds, Shepherdesses, Singers, and Dancers.

SCENE, *BITHYNIA.*

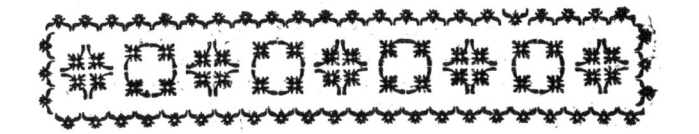

THE SHEEP-SHEARING.

ACT I. SCENE I.

The KING *and* CAMILLO.

CAMILLO.

'TIS now full fixteen years, that I have been
An outcaft, banifh'd man; and though I've found,
Thro' your good grace, a home more hofpitable
Here in *Bithynia*, ftill I'd wifh to lay
My wearied bones within the bofom of
My mother-earth, *Sicilia*.

King. I prithee, good *Camillo*, don't requeft it;
You ftill fhall tarry here to fhare our love.

Cam. Ah! my good lord, *Leontes*
Hath long repented of his tyrant deeds,
Which, thro' ill-grounded jealoufy, defam'd
His virtuous queen, and gave his little babe
(Moft truly his) a prey to rav'ning wolves.

King. Unhappy man!

Cam. But fee the vengeance of the gods! *Antigonus*,
Who undertook t'expofe the harmlefs infant,
Moft juftly perifh'd with it.---Now the king,
Too late convinc'd, and childlefs in his age,
Retires, in cloifter'd folitude to wafte
The weary remnant of his life in tears;

And

And wills me come to share the toils of state,
For him too much, already sunk with woe.

King. But, as thou lov'st me, do not leave me now,
When most we need thy friendship; for thou know'st
How much prince *Forizel*, my son, afflicts me
With the strange courses he of late hath follow'd.
We oft have wonder'd whence arose the change
So visible in thoughts, words, looks, and actions;
Whence blew the sighs, like mildew blasts, to fade
The roses *Hebe* shed upon his cheek;
Whence came that irksomeness of ev'ry joy
Our court affords, and ev'ry beauty there;
Whence, for whole weeks, wou'd he withdraw himself.
Sequester'd, unattended, from the ken
Of ev'ry curious eye; whence that he shut
Out ev'ry friend, that once lodg'd in his heart,
Lest he shou'd know the secret brooding there.

Cam. I oft have thought it strange.

King. But little thinks he
That kings have eyes, piercing as those of *Lynxe*..
His ways are now no longer secret to me;
I've hunted him through all his darkest haunts,
Till, in his kennel, I have earth'd the cub,
Degen'rate boy! to mingle with the mud.

Cam. What means my lord?

King. My good *Camillo*, trust me,
I've had intelligence, the time he steals
From us, from study, and from manly feats,
And exercise of arms, is buried all
Beneath an aged shepherd's sordid roof,
Whose bleating flocks spread o'er that beauteous vale
That winds along the river's side. A stranger,
Here settled in *Bithynia* some few years,
Who yet, beyond th' imagination 'rose
Of all his neighbours, yea from very nothing,
To large possessions, and unnumber'd flocks.

Cam. I've heard of such a man, who hath a daughter
Of note most rare, beyond her low estate.

King. Ay, that's the angle plucks him to his ruin.
Fool! to be caught with such a paltry bait!
A woman's bait!---I could have patience with him,
Meant he to sport it with the am'rous wench,
And had he thriv'd, and, from the wholesome theft,
Had bred a mungril hardy as a mule,
I cou'd have kiss'd the sturdy bastard boy,

As

As he trudg'd barefoot o'er the mountain's brow;
Or smil'd to see his princely sire break forth,
In lording it above the village brats,-----
But, O *Camillo!* where shall I find patience?-----
Thou'lt not believe me, shou'd I swear it true-----
My son, prince *Florizel*, *Bithynia*'s hopes,
My kingdom's heir, this very day intends
To wed the daughter of that base-born clown.

Cam. It is impossible,
A prince to wed a peasant!

King. 'Tis most certain.
But, to confound him past all contradiction,
We mean, at once, to prove and to prevent it.
To-day old *Alcon* (that's her father's name)
Holds an accustom'd rite, sacred to *Pan*,
The god of flocks; it is their shearers feast,
At which he means to solemnize the nuptials
With rural pomp, and pastoral festivity.
But I shall disconcert them, I'll thither,
And thou, *Camillo*, shalt attend me too,
Disguis'd like strangers chance had summon'd there.

Cam. You may dispose me as your grace shall list.
Yet still, I think, the prince, in your report,
Is much abus'd.---I can not think it true.

King. I'll think as thou, till I have prov'd the fact.
[*Exeunt.*

SCENE, *A rural prospect near* ALCON's *house*.

FLORIZEL *and* PERDITA *sitting under a shady tree*.

Flor. These, your unusual weeds, to each part of you
Do give a life; no shepherdess, but *Flora*
Peering in *April*'s front. This, your sheep-shearing,
Is as a meeting of the petty gods,
And you the queen of it.

Perd. My gracious lord, to chide at your extremes,
It not becomes me: O! pardon, that I name them!
Your high self, the kingdom's rising hope,
You have obscur'd with a swain's wearing;
And me, poor humble maid, most goddess like
Prank'd up.

Flor. I bless the time, when my good falcon
Took her flight across thy father's grounds;
Celestial guide, to where my treasure lay.

Per.

The Sheep-Shearing: or

Perd. Now *Jove* afford you caufe! To me, the difference
Forges dread; your greatnefs hath not been us'd
To fear; ev'n now I tremble to think your
Father, by fome accident, fhould pafs this way,
As you did: O! the fates! how would he look
To fee his work, fo noble, vilely bound up:
What wou'd he fay? or how fhould I, in thefe
My borrow'd flaunts, behold the fternnefs of his prefence?

Flor. Apprehend nothing but jollity. The gods
Themfelves, humbling their deities to love,
Have taken the fhapes of beafts upon them.
Jupiter became a bull, and bellowed:
The green *Neptune* a ram, and bleated: And
The fire-rob'd god, golden *Apollo*,
A poor humble fwain, as I feem now.
'Tis our bridal day! Th' affembled gods,
This day, fhow'r rofes down, to deck thy virgin couch!
And love fhall lend the down of his foft wings,
To fmooth thy pillow with eternal joys!
Speak to me, love, and charm me with thy voice.

Perd. No, let me only anfwer you with blufhes:
If I fhould fpeak, you'd think I were too fond;
My tongue's afham'd t'interpret for my heart.

Flor. Hence with referve; it is a foe to love-----
What you tell me is whifper'd to yourfelf.
Virtue and love may harmlefs fport together,
Like little Lambs that wanton on the plain;
While, like a faithful paftor by their fide,
Honour keep off each ravenous defire.

Perd. I think you love me, and think there is
Such virtue fhines about you, that I dare
Intruft mine honour to your faithful love.
Oft, oft, I wifh thou wer't fome peafant fwain,
Born lowly as myfelf; than fhould we live
Unknown, unenvied in our humble ftate,
Content with love beneath the cottage ftraw.

Flor. By heav'n! there's fuch a charm in all thy words,
I wifh I were juft what you'd have me be,
Diftinguifh'd only from the reft by love.
The gueft are come; let's in and entertain
Them chearily, nor think of ought but jollity and love.
[*Exeunt.*

SCENE.

FLORIZL *and* PERDITA.

SCENE, *The Country*,

Enter the KING *and* CAMILLO *habited like old yeomen.*

King. I am certain it cannot be far off, though we have loft our way.

AUTOLICUS *fings without.*

When daffodils begin to peere,
  With hey the doxy over the dale,
Why then comes in the fweet o' th' year;
  For the red blood reigns o'er the winter's pale.

King. We'll afk this merry fellow,
What! hollo! mafter fongfter!

Enter AUTOLICUS.

Aut. Want you me, my mafters? I've got the rareft ballads-----
King. Which is the fhorteft way-----
Aut. The fhorteft way is to hear it out, and then judge for yourfelves.

SINGS.

The lark that 'irra lyra chaunts,
  With hey, with hey, the thrufh and the jay,
Are fummer fongs for me and my aunts,
  As we lie tumbling in the hay.

King. Why, fellow!-----
Aut. Fellow! fellow quoth-a! who made you and I fellows? Do you know who you fpeak to fir?
King. No, truly.
Aut. I thought fo by your manners. I'd have you to know, fir, I have been at court, fir; and have feen the king, fir.
King. I cry you mercy. I did not know you had been fo great a man. And pray how do you like him?
Aut. Why, hum! but fo, fo; fo, fo: And yet he's well enough too; but that he *wants it here* a little. He's not the *wifeft* man in the world; but a damn'd merry fellow for all that, and an excellent companion.

King.

8 *The* Sheep-Shearing : *or*

King. Then you and he have been acquainted.

Aut. As great as cup and can, fir. Lord, lord, I fhall never forget the day that I and he---ha ha ha! 'Twou'd make you die with laughing to fee the old woman foufe the king with a pail of fuds---ha ha ha ! I never fpent fuch a day---But I'll fing you a fong the king made upon that very occafion.

The white fheet bleaching o'er the hedge,
With hey the fweet birds! oh! how they fing!
Doth fet my progging tooth an edge;
For a pot of ale is a difh for a king.

King. Did the king make this?

Aut. I help'd him a little; for, as I faid, he is fome-what dull. He finifh'd the three firft lines, and was damnably fet for a rhime for fing; when I takes up the pot, and flapping him on the back, hit off at once,

For a pot of ale's a difh for a king.

But to fee how he look'd when he found I had drank it all off, ha ha ha! I fhall never forget it, where I to liye a thoufand years: But we had t'other pot, and then compofed t'other fong upon this fame wafh-woman's fair daughter: You fhall hear that too, hem, hem!

SINGS.

T^e linen, by her fingers preft,
Convey'd love's poifon to my breaft;
My heart grew hot, I felt the hurt,
I die, like Herc'les, *by a fhirt;*
Cupid, *to wound, took neither bow nor dart;*
But with her fmoothing-iron fir'd my heart.

Oh ! the king's a rare poet with a little of my help--- The king and I had a hot difpute about the fourth line :

' *I die, like* Herc'les, *by a fhirt.*'

He faid it was a good comparizement for a king; but would not do for a pedlar: Whereof I look'd four, and afk'd, why fo pray? Becaufe, faid he, few pedlar die worth a fhirt. There he had me on the hip, and we both laugh'd fo heartily, that I was obliged to drink off the reft of the beer, or I fhou'd have burft. In troth, he's a good-hu-
mour'd

FLORIZEL *and* PERDITA.

mour'd man, and a pretty poet to my thinking, as poets go now-a-days. Come, you muſt buy it.

King. Nay, ſince 'tis the king's poetry, 'tis fit all his good ſubjects ſhou'd buy it.

Aut. I have no change, maſter.

King. I want none, thou may'ſt keep it all. And now, I pray thee, without further words, which is the neareſt way to the houſe of one *Alcon,* an aged yeoman of good repute, that lives ſomewhere hereabouts?

Aut. Are you going to maſter *Alcon*'s? I'm heartily glad of it; for I ſhall meet you there by and by. There's to be high doings; both a ſheep-ſhearing and a wedding: And, if that will not make ſport enough for one day, I wonder at it. We ſhall not lack for good chear, I warrant you. And I hope to ſell a parcel of my wares.

King. Doſt thou believe it now, *Camillo?*
[*Apart to* Camillo.

Cam. But pray who is to be married there?

Aut. Why, young Mrs. *Perdita,* his daughter; the prettieſt laſs, maſter!---Ods-life! ſhe'll make thy old gums water when thou ſee'ſt her. When you go there, put it about that we may all kiſs the bride; I long dearly to have one ſmack at her ſweet lips.

Cam. And what is he that is deſign'd her huſband?

Aut. Why ſome give out he is a gentleman; but this world is ſo ſtrangly given to lying, that I ſcarce believe a word in ten I hear to any body's advantage; but if he were I am ſure he's nothing the better for that; for I never was acquainted with a gentleman, that is to ſay, to drink with him or ſo, that was not the ſaddeſt dog in nature: Your gentlemen are ſad dogs, ſad dogs, indeed! But this young man has too good a character for a gentleman: Alas! they ſay he has honour and honeſty, and love and virtue, and all that trumpery ſtuff that you never meet with--in gentlemen now-a-days: But it is no matter, *Alcon* hath enough for her and him too, though he were as poor, and as extravagant, as any gentleman of them all.

King. But *Alcon,* I ſuppoſe, knows, for certain, who and what he is to whom he gives his daughter.

Aut. I know not that; 'tis none of my concern.

King. Then pray direct us thither.

Aut. Come here.---Look, you go along this foot-path, (for, if you tread in the graſs, you'll have a quarter-ſtaff over your pate) croſs the ſtile at the end of the meadow, then wind along the river's ſide to where it tumbles and

B   flounces

10 *The* Sheep-Shearing: *or*

flounces down the rock, as white as fillabub; then, turning to the left, mount up the rifing ground, leaving the wood a little to the right, till coming to a fpa‑ cious lawn clofe nibbled by the fheep, as if 'twere fhorn, ftraight on you may defcry old *Alcon's* dwelling; though not a fine, the warmeft hereabouts.---Some bufinefs calls me now another way; but in a hour I'll be with you there.

SINGS.

Jog on, jog on the foot-path way,
 And merrily bend the ftile-a;
A merry heart goes all the day,
 Your fad one tires in a mile-a.

King. Report, *Camillo,* fometimes fpeaks the truth.
To-day the maid is to be wed. To whom
Is yet uncertain; but I think there room
For juft fufpicion that it is my fon.
If fo, th' unhappy object of his love,
Thou beautiful, though perfect innocence,
Muft fall a facrifice to public good.
 Who dares, like *Semele,* to meet a *Jove,*
Should juftly perifh by ambitious love.

[*Exeunt.*

ACT

A C T II.

SCENE, ALCON'S *House.*

The SCENE *discovers* ALCON, FLORIZEL, PERDITA, *the* KING, CAMILLO, *with Shepherds and Shepherdesses.*

ALCON.

WELCOME, kind neighbours, welcome, gentle strangers.
This day we dedicate to mirth and feasting,
You're welcome all: I pray you lack for nothing.
[*Florizel and* Perdita *talk together.*

King. Cou'dst thou believe this, had not thine own
eyes [*Aside* to Camillo.
Borne uncorrupted witness of the truth?

Alcon. Fie, daughter! when my old wife liv'd, upon
This day, she was both pantler, butler, cook;
Both dame and servant; welcom'd all, serv'd all;
Wou'd sing her song, and dance her turn: But you
Retire, as if feasted guest, and not
The hostess of the meeting. Pray you bid
These unknown friends to's welcome; for it is
A way to make us better friends, more known.
Come, quench your blushes, and present yourself
That which you are, mistress o'th' feast. Come on,
And bid us welcome to your sheep-shearing,
As your good flocks shall prosper.

Per. Sirs, you're welcome.
It is my father's will I should take on me
The hostessship o'th' day; you're welcome, sirs.
Give me those flowers, *Dorcas.* Reverend sirs,
For you there's rosemary and rue; these keep
Seeming and favour all the winter long;
Grace and remembrance be unto you both,
And welcome to our shearing.

King. Shepherdefs,
A fair one are you, well you fit our ages
With flowers of winter.

Perd. Sir, the year growing ancient,
Nor yet on fummer's death, nor on the birth
Of trembling winter, the faireft flowers o' th' feafon
Are our carnations and ftreak'd gilliflowers,
Which fome call nature's baftards: of that kind
Our ruftic garden's barren.---Here's for you
Hot lavender, mints, favory, marjoram,
The marygold that goes to bed with th' fun,
And with him rifes weeping; thefe are flowers
Of middle fummer, and, I think, they are given
To men of middle age.---You're very welcome.

Cam. I cou'd leave grazing, were I of your flock,
And only live by gazing.

Perd. Out, alas!
You'd be fo lean, that blafts of *January*
Wou'd blow you through and through. Now, faireft friend,
I wou'd I had fome flowers o' th' fpring, that might
Become your time of day; and your's, and your's,
That wear upon your virgin branches yet
Your maiden blufhes. O *Proferpina*,
For the flow'rs now, that, frighted, thou let'ft fall
From *Dis*'s waggon! Early daffodils,
That come before the fwallow dares, and take
Winds of *March* with beauty; violets dim,
But fweeter than the lids of *Juno*'s eyes,
Or *Cytherea*'s breath; pale primrofes,
That die unmarry'd ere they can behold
Bright *Phœbus* in his ftrength; gold oxflips, and
The crown imperial; lilies of all kinds,
That in the valley grow. O thefe I lack
To make you garlands of, and my fweet friend
To ftrew him o'er and o'er.

Flor. What, like a coarfe?

Perd. No, like a bank for love to lie and play on;
Not like a coarfe; or if,---not'to be buried
But quick, and in mine arms. Come, take your flowers;
Methinks I play, as I have feen them do
In *Whitfund'* paftorals.---I'd make you welcome,
But fear I weary you.

Flor. What e'er you do,
Still better what is done. When you fpeak, fweet,

I'd

FLORIZEL *and* PERDITA.

I'd have you do so ever; when you sing,
I'd have you buy and sell so; so give alms and pray,
In such sweet notes, and, ordering your affairs,
To sing them too; or, when you dance,
Like a smooth wave by gentle winds heav'd up,
So move you to the music's dulcet breath'd,
That I cou'd wish the motion were perpetual.

Perd. O *Doricles*, your praises are to large;
I judge of them as measures of your love,
Not standards of my own worthiness.

King. This is the prettiest low-born lass, that ever
Ran on the green swerd; nothing she does, or seems,
But smacks of something greater than herself,
Too noble for this place.----Had *Florizel*
But thought of bedding without wedding her,
I well cou'd like his liking. [*Apart to* Camillo.

Cam. In good sooth,
She is the very posy of all sweets.

Alc. Come, come, you'd have the pastime to yourselves;
[*to* Florizel *and* Perdita.
But you'll find leisure time enough hereafter
For tales of love. The pastorals begin,
And each one bear his burthen in the song.

Pan, Shepherds, and Sheperdesses enter and sing.

DORCAS SINGS.

Our sheep timely shorn, enriching the swain,
As fresh as the morn, frisk over the plain.
So the generous mind, that with bounty o'erflows,
Feels the heart grows more light, for the good he bestows.

PAN SINGS.

Shepherds hear the voice of Pan,
 God of swains, and rural peace!
I first taught the race of man
 How to shear the woolly fleece:
How your shiv'ring limbs to fold,
Proofs against the winter' cold.

King. I pray, good shepherd, what fair swain is that,
Whose happy hand is to thy daughter's link'd,
Like turtles pair'd, that never mean to part.

Alc. They call him *Dorciles.* He boasts himself
To have a worthy breeding; but I have it
Upon his own report, and I believe him,
He looks like sooth. He says he loves my daughter;
I think so too; for never gaz'd the moon
On the calm ocean, as he'll stand and read
As 'twere my daughter's eyes.---And to be plain,
I think there is not half a kiss to chuse,
Which loves the other best. She e'en wou'd have him,
So let them to't. 'Twere pity cross such love,
And I've enough for both, for she shall bring him
More than he dreams of yet.

Enter a CLOWN.

Clown. O master! did you but hear the pedlar at the door, you wou'd never dance again after a tabor and pipe; no, the bag-pipe cou'd not move you. He sings tunes faster than you can tell money. He utters them as he had eaten ballards.---Then he hath ribbands of all colours in the rainbow, inkles, cambrick, lawns, and garters for the maids, and he sings them over as they were gods and goddesses. You wou'd think a smock were a she angel, he so chaunts to the sleeve-band and the work upon the gusset.

King. Admit him, he's a merry fellow.

Alc. Ay, bring him; we're for all mirth to day.

Enter AUTOLICUS *singing.*

Will you buy any tape, or lace for your cape,
  My dainty duck, my dear---a?
Any silk, any thread, any toys for your head,
  Of the newest and finest fine ware---a?
Come to the pedlar, money's a medler,
That uttereth all men's ware---a.

Clown. What hast thou here? ballads?

Mops. I pray now buy some. I love a ballad or a life in print, for then one is sure they're true.

Aut. Here's one to a very doleful tune, how a usurer's wife was brought to bed of twenty money-bags at a burthen; and how she long'd to eat adders heads and toads carbonado'd.

Mops. But is it true, think you?

Aut.

Florizel and Perdita.

Aut. True, upon my honour. Why do you think, tho' I carry a pack, I'd carry a pack of lies about? here's the midwife's hand to it, one Mrs. *Taleporter*, and six honest wives that were present. I myself saw five young adders creep out of her nostrils and in again at her mouth.

Dor. Bless me from marrying an usurer.

Aut. Here's another ballad of a great huge fish, with eyes like full moons, and twenty rows of teeth as long as plowshares, with a tail like a fiery dragon's, which appear'd upon the coast the 32d of *April*, new stile, breathing flames and brimstone, and vomiting out pin-cushions and love letters. It sung this very ballad against hard-hearted-maids. It was thought this beautiful monster was a woman, and that she was turn'd into an horrible thornback for having pierc'd so many young men's hearts in this world by turning her back upon them, and she now continues a frightful kind of an old fish, call'd a maid. Come, buy it; the ballad's a very pretty, pitiful ballad, and as true as the former.

Dorc. Come, lay it by and shew us another.

Aut. Here's one that I'm sure must please you. It is come from *Italy*, a master-piece of humour, one of your, your, your hurly burlie's, for most people like it, because they do not understand it.

Enter CLOWN.

Clown. O master, here's the rarest news. There are without, I believe, a dozen goat-herds, neat-herds, shepherds, and all sorts, in their holyday jackets, and every man his lass in his hand; they say they have a dance will please plentifully. There's one tight little fellow among them, that, I believe in my conscience, leaps twelve foot and a half from the ground, and he so capers and spins you in the air, you'd swear he was a shuttlecock, and the floor a racket, which, when he touches, sends him up again. Then there's the trimest little black-ey'd wench, so brisk and so frisky, and she doth wink it and splink it at the lad, that, od's my life, I cou'd have found in my heart to have kiss'd the little jade, she look'd so.---They're all without, and only wait for leave to be admitted.

Alc. Away, we'll none of them; here has been too much homely foolery already.---I know, sir, we weary you.

King.

King. You weary thofe that refresh us. I love such gambols much; pray let us fee them.

Clown. O Sir, thefe are none of your common dancers at fairs and----

Alc. Leave your prating; fince thefe good men are pleafed, let them come in.

A Dance of Shepherds and Shepherdeſſes.

Cam. Is it not too far gone? 'tis time to part them.
King. No; I will try both him, and her, and all,
To th' utmoſt proof. It will be time enough
T' unmaſk ourſelves, when they begin the rites.---
I'll make the machine play.---How now, fair ſhepherd!
Your heart is full of fomething, that doth take
Your mind from feaſting. Sooth, when I was young
And handed love, as you do, I was wont
To load my fhe with knacks; I wou'd have ranſack'd
The pedlar's ſilken treaſury, and have pour'd it
To her acceptance. You have let him go,
And nothing marted with him. If your laſs
Interpretation ſhou'd abuſe, and call this
Your lack of love or bounty, you were ſtraited
For a reply at leaſt, if you make a care
Of happy holding her.

Flor. Old fir, I know
She prizes not ſuch trifles as theſe are;
The gifts ſhe looks from me, are pack'd and lock'd
Up in my heart, which I have giv'n already,
But not deliver'd. O, hear me breathe my life
Before this ancient fir, who it ſhould feem
Hath fome time lov'd. I take thy hand, this hand
Soft as the down of *Venus'* doves, and white
As *Ethiopian's* tooth, or the fann'd fnow
That's bolted by the northern blaſt twice o'er.

King. How prettily, young fwain, you feem to waſh
The hand, was white before.----
But to your proteſtation: let me hear
What you profeſs.
Flor. Do, and be witneſs to it.
King. And this my neighbour too.
Flor. And he, and more
Then he, and men; the earth, the heav'ns, and all
The ruling planets, in their circling orbs;
That were I crown'd the moſt imperial monarch,

Thereof

Thereof moft worthy; were I the faireft youth
That ever made eye fwerve; had force and knowledge
More than was ever man's, I wou'd not prize them
Without her love.
 King. Fairly offer'd,
This fhews a found affection.
 Alc. But, my daughter,
Say you the like to him?
 Perd. I cannot fpeak
So well, nothing fo well, no nor mean better.
By the pattern of my own thoughts, I cut out
The purity of his.
 Alc. Call in the prieft.
We'll doubly crown this happy feftival.

Enter PRIEST, *with* AUTOLICUS *officioufly attending him.*

And friends unknown, you fhall bear witnefs to it.
Obferve the young man well, and note him fo,
That in what garb hereafter you may fee him,
Still may you paint his features in your mind,
And in remembrance bear his facred vows.----
I give my daughter to him [*hands her to the Prieft*] and will make
Her portion equal his.
 Flor. O that muft be
I' th' virtue of thy daughter; one being dead
I fhall have more than you can guefs at yet,
Enough then for your wonder.
 Aut. [*to the King.*] Mafter Greybeard, hark you, a word with you; be fure you remember to let us all have a kifs at the bride.
 King. O fear it not; when they are marry'd you fhall kifs the bride.
 Flor. Come on; why do you now delay my blifs?
Moft holy father, do thine office now,
Before thefe witneffes.
 Prieft. My fon, thine hand;
And, daughter, thine.
 King. Soft, fir, a while; befeech you,
Have you a father?
 Flor. I have; but what of him?
 King. Knows he of this?
 Flor. He neither does, nor fhall.

C

King.

King. Methinks a farther
Is, at the nuptials of his son, a guest
That best becomes the table. Pray you once more,
Is not your father grown incapable
Of reasonable affairs? Is he not stupid
With age, and alt'ring rheums? Can he speak, hear,
Know man from man, dispute his own estate?
Lies he not bed-rid, and again plays o'er
The follies of his childhood?

Flor. No, good sir,
He hath his health, and ampler strength, indeed,
Than most have at his age.

King. By my white beard,
You offer him, if this be so, a wrong
Something unfilial. Reason, my son,
Shou'd chuse himself a wife; but as good reason,
The father (all whose joy is nothing else
But fair posterity) shou'd hold some counsel
In such a business.

Flor. I yield all this;
But, for some other reasons, my grave sir,
Which 'tis not fit you know, I not acquaint
My father of this business.

King. Let him know it.
Flor. He shall not.
King. Pr'ythee let him.
Flor. No, he must not.
King. Let him, my son; he shall not need to grieve
At knowing of thy choice.

Flor. Come, come, he must not,
You interrupt us, sir; no more of this,
But mark our vows.

King. Mark your divorce, young sir,
 [*discovers himself.*
Whom son I blush to call; thou art too base
To be acknowledg'd. Thou, a scepter's heir,
That thus affect'st a sheephook! thou, old traitor,
I'm sorry that, by hanging thee, I can
But shorten thy life one week. And thou fresh piece
Of excellent witchcraft, who, of force, must know
The royal fool thou cop'st with--- [*Turning to* Florizel.

Perd. Will't please you, sir, begone.
I told you what would come of this! beseech you
Of your own state take care. This dream of mine,
Being now awake, I'll queen it no inch farther,

But

FLORIZEL *and* PERDITA. 19

But milk my ewes, and weep.
King. By heav'n he knows me, yet he blushes not.
Flor. What blush to love! Shame light on him that
does.
I glory in't; for 'tis the next approach
Of mortal souls to the divine perfection.
King. I tax not love, but thy degen'rate choice.
Flor. Can you look there, and yet arraign my choice?
No; 'tis the will of heav'n she shou'd be lov'd,
And it were impious pride to contradict it.
King. Hell! death and furies! dost thou still persist?
Flor. Persist to death.---My *Perdita*, my love,
Let not affliction change that lovely cheek.
I've sworn, and will be thine till death.
King. And thou shalt keep thy vow.---*Camillo*, call
Our guards, and lead this forc'ress, and her sire,
To instant death.
Flor. I charge you, sir, forbear,
By heav'n, the first that touches her shall die.
King. Resistance is in vain. There waits without
An armed force full fifty times your strength.
Aut. O blood! I shall be hang'd too for the damn'd lies
I told him of himself [*Aside.*
King. For thee, fond boy, if I but see thee sigh,
We will cut off the hopes of thy succession;
Not hold thee of our blood.
Flor. From my succession wipe me; I shall be
Heir to her love, and reign within her heart.
Cam. This, sir, is madness.
Flor. Call it what you will,
To barter shew for happiness is gain.
Not for *Bithynia*, nor the pomp that may
Be thereout glean'd, for all the sun sees, or
The close earth wombs, or the profound seas hide
In unknown fathoms, will I break my faith
Plighted to this my fair, beloved bride.
Perd. You have:
I cannot answer you with aught, but tears.
Alc. Most gracious king, if thou'lt vouchsafe to hear
A wretch, whom once you honour'd with your friendship,
As did *Camillo*, hearken to *Antigonus*. [*Discovers himself.*
King. Antigonus.
Cam. How, risen from the dead!
King. 'Tis he indeed
If my own senses vouch the wond'rous truth,

C 3 'Twas

'Twas faid thou wer't devour'd by hungry wolves.
Alc. So has it been for fixteen years believ'd.
King. Whence then this myftry how cam'ft thou hither!
Alc. You may remember our diftemper'd king
Leontes growing jealous of his queen,
Far gone with child, moft barbaroufly doom'd
To be expos'd, the infant fhe fhou'd bear.
I undertook the cruel tafk, through mercy,
Firft vowing to myfelf to fave the babe,
And fly with it to fome more peaceful fhore.
Entring the wood, with this determination,
I fpy'd the carcafs of a man, juft newly
Slain, and but half devour'd by a wolf.
On this I put my cloaths, and near it ftrew'd
The infant's little weeds all fmear'd with blood,
Which being found, and known, 'twas thought by all
That we were both devoured by wild beafts.
Then flying with my little charge, I came to feek
An hofpitable fhelter in *Bithynia*.----
How well my ward in fixteen years hath grown,
Turn there, and you may fee.
Flor. My *Perdita*.
Alc. My lord, I knew that *Doricles* was *Florizel*,
Elfe fhou'd he not, however good and kind,
Have leave to look upon her royal beauties.
Take her my lord.---In truth, fhe is a treafure
More worth than all the riches of the eaft:
For fhe'th been bred, unknowing of her ftate,
With virtues that may well adorn a throne;
And, in herfelf, fo fweet her difpofition,
You wou'd think mercy, charity, and peace,
Come down from heav'n, and lodg'd within her breaft.
My child, my child, thou'rt now my child no more;
Yet don't forget, that once you call'd me father.
Perd. Ne'er fhall thou meet lefs reverence and love
Then heretofore, but much more gratitude.
King. Since thou haft loft one father, gentleft maid
'Tis fitting I provide thee with another.
Give me thy hand, my fon; here take thy *Perdita*,
And may the gods fhower bleffings on you both.
Flor. I am all tranfport, extacy, and rapture:
O let me fall, and kifs your royal feet.
[*Kneels to the King.*
And you, my *Perdita*.

Perd.

FLORIZEL and PERDITA.

Perd. That you are mine, I joy, howe'er it be;
But no lefs truly fhou'd I joy, had you
Fall'n to my ftate, than that I rife to yours.

Cam. Now, to confirm thy joy, *Antigonus*,
Leontes, fatisfy'd his queen was virtuous,
For many years has mour'd his infant loft,
Depriv'd of ev'r child. And now thy *Perdita*
Is only heirefs of *Sicilia*'s crown.

All. Joy, joy to *Perdita* and *Florizei*.

Aut. [*kneeling to* Perdita.] O! my good lady princefs, let the joy be univerfal; leave not a wrinkled brow, or cloudy face, in all the realm upon this happy day; begin your reign with gracelefs act of mercy; intreat the good king, your worthy father-in-law, to forgive me all the damn'd lies I told him of himfelf. I own I have been a very great rogue, and deferve hanging; but I will mend my life, and promife that I will not never do the like no more. Oh! ho! [*Cries.*

Perd. May I prefume to fue for mercy for him?

King. He needs it not; he is a pleafant knave,
And ne'er offended us.---Be merry firrah,

Aut. Huzza! huzza! huzza! --- [*Leaps about.*] a reprieve, a reprieve. But may it pleafe your grace---he, he, he!---I hope you don't forget your promife, he, he, he! that when they were marry'd, I fhou'd kifs the bride.

King. And fo thou fhalt; I'll fet thee an example.
[*Kiffes her.*

Aut. [*kiffes her.*] This is the firft time I ever kifs'd a princefs. [*Snatches another kifs.*] And this fhall be the laft. By *Jupiter*, I think I feel myfelf infpir'd; and if all your majefties will give me leave, I'll fing you a fong I have made extrumpery on the occafion.

S I N G S.

Then let us all be blithe and gay
Upon this joyful, bridal day.
That FLORIZEL *weds* PERDITA,
That FLORIZEL *weds* PERDITA.
And let each nymph and fhepherd tell
No happy pair e'er lov'd fo well,
As PERDITA *and* FLORIZEL.
As PERDITA *and* FLORIZEL.

C H O R U S.

CHORUS.

Sing high, sing down, sing ding-dong bell,
For PERDITA *and* FLORIZEL.

FINIS.